ENCOUNTER!
Receive Christ's Freedom

Joel Comiskey

Published by CCS Publishing

www.cellchurchsolutions.com

Published by CCS Publishing
23890 Brittlebush Circle
Moreno Valley, CA 92557 USA
1-888-344-CELL

Cover design by Josh Talbot
Editing by Scott Boren

All Scripture quotations, unless otherwise indicated, are from the Holy Bible, New International Version, Copyright ©1973, 1978, 1984 by International Bible Society. Used by
permission.

CCS Publishing is the book-publishing division of Cell Church Solutions, a resource and
coaching ministry dedicated to equipping leaders for cell-based ministry.
Find us on the World Wide Web at **www.CellChurchSolutions.com**

Publisher's Cataloging-in-Publication
 (Provided by Quality Books, Inc.)

   Comiskey, Joel, 1956-
      Encounter! : receive Christ's freedom / by Joel
   Comiskey.
      p. cm.
      Includes bibliographical references and index.
      ISBN 0975581929

      1. Spiritual life--Christianity.
      2. Self-actualization (Psychology)--Religious aspects--
   Christianity. 3. Spiritual formation. I. Title.

   BV4501.3.C6552 2007   248.4
                        QBI06-600330

Table of Contents

Introduction. 5

Lesson 1: Encountering God. 7

Lesson 2: Receiving God's Forgiveness. 17

Lesson 3: Forgiving Others 25

Lesson 4: The Power of the Cross Over Sin and Satan 33

Lesson 5: The Power of the Cross to Heal Emotional Wounds. . . 4 1

Lesson 6: The Power the Cross Over Strongholds. 51

Lesson 7: The Power of the Cross Over Sickness and Death. . . 63

Lesson 8: Living in Victory 69

Appendix One: How to Coach Someone using this Material. . . . 79

Appendix Two: Instructions on Leading an Encounter Retreat 83

Appendix Three: Spiritual Inventory 85

Index. 89

Introduction

This book will help overcome those areas of sin that weigh you down in your Christian life. The first time I studied similar "Encounter material" Jesus pinpointed areas of anger, ungodliness, and Satanic strongholds in my own life. He set me free and showed me how important an Encounter with God event is. Previous to that encounter in April 2000, I thought such training was commendable. Afterwards, I strongly recommended that everyone in the church study it.

God wants you to be free from all sin—from any addiction or bondage. Keep this in mind as you work through this book. The writer of Hebrews declares, "…. let us throw off everything that hinders and the sin that so easily entangles, and let us run with perseverance the race marked out for us" (12:1).

Some believe that holiness means legalism. They think holiness is an old, useless idea—it is all about what you should not do, not what you can do. "I only dwell on God's love and grace," they say. Yet God's grace always leads to true freedom, which is holiness. If it doesn't, it's not the real thing. Scripture says, "For the grace of God that brings salvation has appeared to all men. It teaches us to say 'No' to ungodliness and worldly passions, and to live self-controlled, upright and godly lives in this present age" (Titus 3:11–12). God's grace teaches us to say no to addictions, sinful habits, and bondages. The result is holiness. Holiness equals wholeness. Jesus leads us down the path of holiness where freedom and truth are found.

If you're working through this book alone, you would benefit from time with a coach who can help you, answer your questions, and hold you accountable. In the appendix, you'll find tips for coaches.

Additional resources

Encounter! is part of a five-book series that prepares someone to become a mature follower of Jesus Christ. If you are interested in the other four books in this series, you may purchase them at www.cellchurchsolutions.com or by calling 1-888-344-CELL.

Many churches will teach this material in a group setting. This is a great way to use this Encounter material. Teaching outlines and PowerPoints are provided for all five equipping books in this series on CD. Purchase this CD at the CCS web site or by calling the toll free number. Appendix 2 does offer some help in hold an Encounter retreat but the CD offers much more.

Encountering God

Someone tried to figure out how Moses could have cared for the multitude of Israelites in the desert after their Exodus from Egypt (Exodus 11:21). This person calculated that they would have needed 1500 tons of food a day, 11,000,000 gallons of water, and a daily camping ground that would cover the size of Rhode Island (approx. 750 square miles).

I don't think Moses sat down to figure out the logistics of what God told him to do before he left Egypt. He had faith that God would take care of everything. The Bible says, "The LORD would speak to Moses face to face, as a man speaks with his friend" (Exodus 33:11). God's miraculous power must have also boosted the confidence of Moses. God performed wonders and miracles not seen before or after—water out of rocks, guiding fire by night and cloud by day, manna appearing on the ground, and quail flying into camp as food.

Yet, God also disciplined Moses, as a father or mother disciplines their children. Moses learned important lessons on what pleased God and how to approach Him. Some of these lessons are laid out for us in Exodus 33-34 as Moses prepared to meet God on Mount Sinai.

Preparation for an encounter with God

Moses longed for God. He wanted to know God intimately. In Exodus 33:18 Moses says, "… show me your glory." Moses expected God to act and show Himself.

To truly encounter God you need to ask God to reveal Himself so you can know Him better. Ask yourself, "What am I expecting God to do as I read the pages of this book? God wants to change and transform you. Allow Him to work miracles in your life, as He did with Moses. Expect Him to manifest Himself and show you His glory. The first principle, therefore, is expectancy.

God has expectations and objectives for you that far exceed your own. He wants to transform and heal you even in areas you don't know about yet. In Isaiah 55:9 God says, "As the heavens are higher than the earth, so are my ways higher than your ways and my thoughts than your thoughts." Be open for those things He will reveal.

He will surprise you by answering your prayers them in a far greater way than you expect. Ephesians 3:20 says, "Now to him who is able to do immeasurably more than all we ask or imagine, according to His power that is at work within us." The Message paraphrase of the Bible says it more graphically, "God can do anything, you know—far more than you could ever imagine or guess or request in your wildest dreams! He does it not by pushing us around but by working within us, his Spirit deeply and gently within us." Ask God to work supernaturally in your life. Ask Him to renew you and fill you. Ask Him to do mighty things—things that you never thought were possible.

The second principle, the principle of participation is found in Exodus 34:1–2. God said to Moses, "Be ready in the morning, and then come up on Mount Sinai. Present yourself to me there on top of the mountain." God asked Moses to get ready for the encounter. You'll get from this Encounter as much as you are willing to give. As you read this book, commit yourself to obey God's will in your life. Remember what God said in the book of Jeremiah, "You will seek me and find me when you seek me with all your heart" (Jeremiah 29:13).

Try IT!

Read Acts 1:14.
What were the disciples doing as they waited for the Holy Spirit to come at Pentecost?

_____

_____

What can you do to prepare yourself for an encounter with God?

_____

_____

_____

_____

_____

God is always ready to bless those who seek Him. Notice how willing Jesus was to heal those who approached Him with sincere hearts. A man with leprosy, for example, approached Jesus saying, "'Lord, if you are willing, you can make me clean.' Jesus reached out his hand and touched the man. 'I am willing,' he said. 'Be clean!' Immediately he was cured of his leprosy" (Matthew 8:2).

All God wants you to do is seek Him and humble yourself before Him. His response will be beyond your expectations.

The third principle is Intimacy. In Exodus 34:3 God said to Moses, "No one is to come with you or be seen anywhere on the mountain; not even the flocks and herds may graze in front of the mountain" Like Moses, God wants to meet you personally and intimately. He already knows everything about you, so there's nothing you can hide from Him. Hebrews 4:13 says, "Nothing in all creation is hidden from God's sight. Everything is uncovered and laid bare before the eyes of him to whom we must give account."

Try IT!

In your own words, define the meaning of each word as they relate to encountering God:

Expectancy: _____

_____

_____

Participation: _____

_____

_____

Intimacy: _____

_____

_____

God's plan for you

In Genesis we find the story of a man named Abram (Abraham). God gave Abraham two key promises. The first promise was to make him a great nation. "The LORD said to Abram, 'Leave your country, your people and your father's household and go to the land I will show you. I will make you into a great nation and I will bless you; I will make your name great, and you will be a blessing. I will bless those who bless you, and whoever curses you I will curse; and all peoples on earth will be blessed through you'" (Genesis 12:1–3).

Secondly, God gave Abraham the land (Genesis 13: 14–17): "The LORD said to Abram after Lot had parted from him, 'Lift up your eyes from where you are and look north and south, east and west. All the land that you see I will give to you and your offspring forever. I will make your offspring like the dust of the earth, so that if anyone could count the dust, then your offspring could be counted. Go, walk through the length and breadth of the land, for I am giving it to you.'" The promise of the land gave Abraham peace and confidence, knowing that God had a perfect plan for him.

Like Abraham, God has plans of blessing and peace for your life. Since the moment you were conceived, God has been working to reveal that perfect plan and even now He's preparing you for it. God said to His people, "For I know the plans I have for you," declares the LORD, "plans to prosper you and not to harm you, plans to give you hope and a future" (Jeremiah 29:11). During this encounter, know that God is for you and not against you. He has your best interests in mind.

Try IT!

Read Isaiah 48:18–19.
What would have happened to God's children if they had listened to God?

_____

_____

_____

Write down what you believe God wants to do in your life as you listen and obey Him:

_____

_____

_____

_____

_____

_____

_____

Sealing God's promises

After Abraham had heard God's promises, he built an altar to honor God. Genesis 12:8 says, "From there he [Abraham] went on toward the hills east of Bethel and pitched his tent … There he built an altar to the Lord and called on the name of the Lord." On another occasion, Genesis 13:18 says, "So Abram moved his tents and went to live near the great trees of Mamre at Hebron, where he built and altar to the LORD." The altar was a group of stones that represented Abraham's response to the promises of God.

In our day, we don't pile up stones to build an altar, but we should respond to God's work and promises in a special way. Building an altar shows our hope and faith in God as we respond to His promises and words for our life. You'll build an altar as you present your requests before God, believing that He will answer.

Try IT!

True or false:
- ☐ God requires us to make a physical altar to show our commitment.
- ☐ God looks for the response of the heart.
- ☐ The Old Testament has no application for us today.

People God touched

God is in the business of changing lives for the better. Scripture gives us many examples of how He does this.

Jacob was one of the two sons of Isaac. He deceived his brother Esau for his Father's special blessing. Jacob had to flee for his life when Esau found out. His life on the run was full of disappointment. Many years later when he was about to meet his brother, who he thought wanted to kill him, Jacob had an encounter with God. Genesis 32:30 says, "So Jacob called the place Peniel, saying, 'It is because I saw God face to face, and yet my life was spared.'" During that encounter, God changed Jacob's identity (Genesis 32:28) and gave him a new perspective (Genesis 33:10). God wants to give you a new identity and a right perspective for your life. As you encounter God, He will work wonders in your life.

Try IT!

Write out your own prayer, asking Jesus to prepare you to meet Him.

_____

_____

_____

_____

_____

_____

_____

Even the great King David needed to encounter God. At one point in his life, David committed adultery and then murder when he sent the woman's husband off to war where David knew he would be killed. David acknowledged his sin and asked God to work deeply in his life, "Then I acknowledged my sin to you and did not cover up my iniquity. I said, 'I will confess my transgressions to the Lord'—and you forgave the guilt of my sin" (Psalm 32:5). David experienced God's grace and acceptance. He said, "The sacrifices of God are a broken spirit; a broken and contrite heart, O God, you will not despise" (Psalm 51:17).

In the New Testament, Jesus encountered a woman in Samaria who had a sinful past that hung over her. At the moment of her encounter with Jesus, her life was in disarray (John 4:17–18). Yet Jesus transformed her. Scripture says, "Many of the Samaritans from that town believed in Him because of the woman's testimony" (John 4:39–42). God wants to transform you. He wants to do exceedingly and abundantly more than you could ask or imagine.

> ## Memorize IT!
> Psalm 32:5: "Then I acknowledged my sin to you and did not cover up my iniquity. I said, 'I will confess my transgressions to the Lord'—and you forgave
> the guilt of my sin"

Everyone needs to have an encounter with God

The Bible tells us how to encounter God. Like Moses, we need to expect God to reveal Himself. God asks for our participation, and we need to keep in mind that we alone will give an account to Him.

Like Jacob, perhaps you need to leave your past behind, change your identity, and ask God to transform your character. Or perhaps you need healing from wounds, emotional stability, and a new reputation—like the Samaritan woman. Or, like David, maybe you need a new heart, a new spirit, and the joy that comes from God's forgiveness.

> ### Do IT!
> *Tell God what you're expecting from this Encounter.*
> *Ask Him to begin that special work in your life.*

A relationship with Jesus takes a lifetime of getting to know each other. It's not a ritual you perform. Nor is the prayer you prayed the goal; rather it's the place where you begin.

God is able to do exceedingly and abundantly more than we can ask or imagine. He's in the business of transformation. If you allow Him, He'll transform you and make you a whole person. Abraham made a physical altar to God in response to the promises he received. Like Abraham, you should respond to God's work in your life by allowing Him to work freely and fully in you.

Realize that God desires to heal you of any and all bondages, whether they are addictions, unforgiveness, curses, negative childhood experiences, or guilt. Only when we are free from the weight of sin and past hurts can we begin to soar like the eagle to new heights of victory and power. Hebrews 12:1–2 says, "Let us throw off everything that hinders and the sin that so easily entangles, and let us run with perseverance the race marked out for us. Let us fix our eyes on Jesus, the author and perfecter of our faith."

Remember IT!

What stood out to you in this lesson?_____

_____

_____

_____

_____

_____

_____

_____

Main points:
1. God wants to have an encounter with you.
2. Your role is to prepare your heart, expect God to do great things, and participate. He'll do the rest.

Apply IT!

1. Take a few moments to think about what you would like God to do as you read this book. Expect God to work in those areas.
2. Pray a prayer like the following for each person you must forgive:
   Heavenly Father, I choose to forgive _____ *[person's name] for* _____ *[name of offense]. This situation has made me feel* _____ *[describe the feeling]."*

Receiving God's Forgiveness

Do you ever feel weighed down by your past failures? It could be the accumulated burden of many wrong turns or the heavy load of one significant transgression. Regardless, the strain becomes tiresome. Here is some great news: "You do not have to continue to drag that junk around!" God's forgiveness is an opportunity to be released from that burden.

Listen to this story Jesus told. There was a reckless son who asked his father for his inheritance. When it was given, the son wasted it on one wrong choice after another. The son soon found himself penniless, living and eating with the pigs and desperately wanting to change his circumstances. At that point, he decided to humble himself and go back to his father. He said to himself, "I will say to him, Father, I have sinned against heaven and against you" (Luke 15:18). The son seriously doubted his Father's acceptance, but Scripture says, "But while he was still a long way off, his Father saw him and was filled with compassion for him; he ran to his son, threw his arms around him and kissed him" (Luke 15:20).

God responds to us in the same way today. He welcomes back His children. He's ready to receive, forgive, and bless those who turn back to Him.

As you are open and honest with God, He'll graciously receive and heal you. God's plan is that we walk in a right relationship with Him. That relationship involves repentance and forgiveness.

The process of forgiveness—repentance

You'll notice how the reckless son didn't try to cover up his need. Repentance is simply acknowledging that God is right, admitting sin, and returning to Him.

God always has His hands outstretched and is more than willing to hear our prayer to Him. Isaiah 59:1 says, "Surely the arm of the LORD is not too short to save, nor his ear too dull to hear. But your iniquities have separated you from your God."

The first step of true repentance, therefore, is to realize that the offense is primarily against God. Each sin must be dealt with to clear the way for a right relationship with Him. I'm referring to the desire to change the attitudes, thoughts, or actions that offend God. David said, "Against you, you only, have I sinned and done what is evil in your sight" (Psalm 51:4).

The second step is to confess the sins one by one. David said about his sin: "Search me, O God, and know my heart; test me and know my anxious thoughts. See if there is any offensive way in me, and lead me in the way everlasting" (Psalm 139:23–24). As God reveals areas of your life that are not pleasing to Him, confess them and renounce them. Ask God to break any bondage in your life that was caused by sin. Jesus said, "I tell you the truth, everyone who sins is a slave to sin … if the Son sets you free, you will be free indeed" (John 8:34, 36).

Try IT!

Fill in the blanks:
1. Realize the offense is against _____.
2. Confess the _____ one by one.
3. Ask God to _____ that particular area of your life.

The third step is to ask God to transform that particular area of your life. Ask Jesus to turn your weakness into strength. Romans 12:1–2 says, "Therefore, I urge you, brothers, in view of God's mercy, to offer your bodies as living sacrifices, holy and pleasing to God—this is your spiritual act of worship. Do not conform any longer to the pattern of this world, but be transformed by the renewing of your mind." Always remember that God's ultimate purpose for you is transformation.

Try IT!

According to verse 19, where do these sins come from?

_____

_____

Which of the sins listed here do you have to deal with?

_____

_____

_____

_____

_____

_____

Accept God's forgiveness

So many people live in bondage because they don't receive the free forgiveness that God offers them. They live a life of guilt, thinking that God might forgive some sins but will then demand retribution for other sins. Yet Scripture says this about God: [He is the one] "who forgives all your sins and heals all your diseases, who redeems your life from the pit and crowns you with love and compassion" (Psalm 103:3, 4).

God knows our frailty and inability to earn our right standing by human effort. That's why He sent His Son Jesus to pay the price for our sins. Scripture says, "We all, like sheep, have gone astray, each of us has turned to his own way; and the Lord has laid on Him the iniquity of us all" (Isaiah 53:6). Jesus paid the price for your sins with His own blood. You can receive God's forgiveness through Jesus Christ.

Try IT!

Read 1 John 1:9.
What does this verse say to those who confess their sins?

_____

_____

_____

What hinders you from receiving God's forgiveness?

_____

_____

_____

_____

_____

_____

_____

The same Jesus who died on the cross for our sins offers forgiveness in each area of our lives. We simply must receive God's forgiveness in each area of our lives.

Memorize IT!
Romans 8:31–32: "What, then, shall we say in response to this? If God is for us, who can be against us? He who did not spare his own Son, but gave him up for us all— how will he not also, along with him, graciously give us all things?"

Hindrances to receiving God's forgiveness

Many people won't forgive themselves because they base forgiveness on good works. They feel disappointed in their own performance and the natural consequence is to try and pay for those shortcomings by doing more good things than bad things. The result is guilt and self-condemnation as those feelings of unworthiness persist. People beat themselves up while living in doubt. Many continue to live this way, never feeling worthy of God's love.

Try IT!
True or false:
☐ God's forgiveness is dependent on our good works.
☐ God's forgiveness is based on His love and grace.
☐ Receiving God's forgiveness brings healing.

Perhaps you've felt this way. God wants you to accept His forgiveness in every area of you life. By not accepting God's forgiveness, you're saying that Christ's death on the cross isn't sufficient. Yes, God does demand payment for sin, but Jesus has already paid the price for your sin and has diverted God's wrath. It is finished. Believe it and receive it. One man died for all, so that you can go free.

When a person fully accepts Christ's sacrifice on the cross as the once and for all payment for sin, freedom is the result.

Another hindrance to not receiving God's forgiveness is failure to understand human finiteness. Let's face it, we are human and imperfect, inclined to make mistakes. We must forgive ourselves by receiving the truth that God has forgiven us, especially when we feel guilt for past sins, wrong decisions, or lost opportunities.

I had one roommate who would never forgive himself for passing up the opportunity to marry a particular woman. He carried around past guilt for missing God's will—or so he thought. God is bigger than our mistakes. He doesn't want us to live with our guilt and burdens. Jesus says in Matthew 11:28–30, "Come to me, all you who are weary and burdened, and I will give you rest. Take my yoke upon you and learn from me, for I am gentle and humble in heart, and you will find rest for your souls. For my yoke is easy and my burden is light."

Stop for a moment and picture that promise happening in your life. Then, let that vision of rest and freedom from your past motivate you to trust God and believe that He loves you.

Do IT!
Read Romans 15:7 and then simply believe that God loves you and forgives you. Stop striving and believe that God accepts you

Let's accept the fact that we are finite and imperfect. Only God never fails or never makes a mistake. It is not necessary for us to make excuses for our shortcomings or to be defensive because we are not perfect.

Remember IT!
Write out a prayer asking God to help you understand and apply one thing from this lesson

_____

_____

_____

_____

_____

_____

Main points:

1. Repentance is a change of mind and direction. It involves confession of sin, turning from self, and living to please God.
2. Many people are in bondage because they don't accept the fact that God loves them and is waiting to forgive them.

Apply IT!

1. If you have a problem with receiving God's forgiveness, recognize the problem and repent. You may pray a prayer like this: "Father, I recognize that I haven't received Your forgiveness. I repent of my failure to believe in all that You've done for me on the cross. I now receive Your forgiveness."
2. Be sure to reaffirm your confidence by saying, "Father, I reaffirm my confidence and faith in Your Word" (read Psalm 103:12).
3. Then confess your freedom as an act of faith: "Father, as an act of my will, I will receive Your forgiveness and believe it is sufficient because You have forgiven me. From this moment I believe I'm liberated from past bondages, and I ask You to fill me with Your Spirit.".

Forgiving Others

Do you ever struggle with the effects of a person who has hurt you deeply? Maybe you experience inner turmoil when you see that person or think of that time. Now imagine if that soul wrenching was gone. Think of no longer being plagued by the past and then arriving at a place where you actually desire good things for the person who hurt you. God wants release you from that burden and pain!

This has happened in my life. In 1985 while I was a single pastor of a new church plant called Hope Alliance, I desperately longed for affirmation in the midst of struggles and success in spite of the obstacles. One day I received a phone call from Anne, one of the members. I figured she needed counseling or prayer. I was shocked when Anne directed her complaints against me, telling me that I was a failure, that no one liked me, and that it was best if she found another church. Her words cut deep into my sensitive soul. The hurt soon turned into bitterness. I was filled with resentment the next day as I drove from Long Beach, CA to Fresno, CA to attend an Evangelism Explosion conference. I remember dwelling on her words during that long, restless drive. Right outside Fresno the bitterness reached a boiling point. I stopped the car and cried out to God.

At that moment I heard God clearly whisper, "Joel, if you're not willing to forgive Anne, neither will I forgive you your sins." I opened my Bible and read these words of Jesus, "For if you forgive men when they sin against you, your heavenly Father will also forgive you. But if you do not forgive men their sins, your Father will not forgive your sins" (Matthew. 6:14). I wrestled with God. How could I forgive this woman who wronged me and wounded me so deeply? Yet, I also realized that I couldn't live life filled with bitterness. God won that afternoon. I gave my unforgiveness and bitterness to Jesus and He took the burden. I even enjoyed the conference. When I returned to Long Beach, I discovered that Anne was a deeply wounded person and her remarks reflected that hurt. Often we don't know why people react and hurt us. But God still calls us to forgive

Forgive others

Jesus says that unless we forgive, He won't forgive us. I remember when God riveted this verse on my soul. Jesus said, "For if you forgive men when they sin against you, your heavenly Father will also forgive you" (Matthew 6:14). We've already talked about receiving God's forgiveness, but if we're not ready to forgive those who sin against us, we shut off the flow of God's love and grace toward us. We must forgive.

Try IT!
List specific hurts from your past for which you carry unforgiveness:

_____

_____

_____

_____

_____

_____

_____

_____

Unforgiveness is a bad option

Injustice is everywhere. People are hurt all the time, and often it's not their fault. Some people rebound from the tragedies while others sink lower into a pit of despair and bitterness. Their hearts become hardened.

If anyone deserved to hold bitterness, it was a Biblical character named Joseph. Joseph had to work through the death of his mother (Gen. 35:19), and also face his brothers' hatred (Gen. 37:4). They tried to kill him but ended up selling him to a band of slave traders who were on their way to Egypt. If that wasn't enough, in Egypt Joseph was again betrayed—this time by the wife of the master of the house. She accused him of adultery (Gen. 37:12–36). He languished in prison due to this false accusation. Then in prison Pharaoh's principal official promised to help him get out (Gen. 39–40). That hope was again crushed by the official's forgetfulness.

Through all the pain and suffering, Joseph kept his focus on God's love and grace. He never allowed his heart to become hard. And through all the trials, God had a plan. He lifted up Joseph to become second in command to the Pharaoh (Genesis 41).

The key lesson that we can learn about Joseph is that he never allowed the venom of bitterness to fill him and poison his life. When God lifted Joseph up, he could freely lead and give of himself. Just like Joseph, we live in a sinful and unjust world, full of pain, abandonment, abuse, fear, prejudices, discrimination, hurt, loneliness, rejection, resentment, and anger.

You might be struggling with those who have wronged you. But remember the words of Jesus, "And when you stand praying, if you hold anything against anyone, forgive him, so that your Father in heaven may forgive you your sins" (Mark 11:25).

Try IT!

Read Ephesians 4:32.
How are we to act toward one another?

_____

_____

_____

In what area of your life do you struggle with unforgiveness?

_____

_____

_____

_____

_____

_____

_____

What does it mean to forgive?

I served in a church in which a key pastor committed a moral failure that drove dozens and dozens from the church. This pastor confessed his sin to the church, and I continued to work with him. My new relationship with him, however, was different. I didn't have the same trust and confidence in him, because I wondered if it could happen again. Before his fall, I was impressed when he freely shared his spiritual dryness and lack of time with God. After his fall, I became concerned when he shared such things. My trust barometer had gone way down.

Remember that to forgive and trust are not the same. We must forgive, but trust often takes time to rebuild. Trust, in fact, is not always restored, but we must always forgive. Forgiving someone else is actually doing ourselves a favor. It releases us from pain, hurtful memories, and anger. Living with bitterness tears holes in our soul. Often unwanted physical symptoms develop.

We must forgive to stay free from slavery and bondage. Forgiving others liberates us from negative emotions and feelings. The actual Greek word "forgive" means to send away, to liberate, to cancel. When you forgive, you recognize the pain the sin caused. You also calculate what the other person has taken from you. But then you must mentally release the person.

How do you know when you've forgiven someone?

This is a tough question that isn't easily answered. But it doesn't mean forgetting the offense. It's practically impossible to forget memories of past hurts.

Forgiveness, rather, is measured by whether you actively cherish the bad feeling that comes from the memory. If someone has hurt you, you need to release that person each time the bad memory comes to your mind. And most likely there will be numerous times. Not just once or twice. Anne's offense (mentioned in the introduction) popped in my mind numerous times after I forgave her, but I referred back to my commitment of releasing her.

Try IT!

Have you released (forgiven) those who have hurt you in the past?

_____

_____

_____

_____

Do IT!

Ask the Holy Spirit to give you the power to forgive (e.g., stop cherishing the bad feeling that comes from the memory).

Jesus offers victory

Most likely someone or something has wounded you. Also remember that you've wounded others at some time. The good news is that Jesus Christ offers forgiveness and healing for all sins and offenses. In referring to Jesus Christ, Isaiah 61:1–3 says, "The Spirit of the Sovereign LORD is on me, because the LORD has anointed me to preach good news to the poor. He has sent me to bind up the brokenhearted, to proclaim freedom for the captives and release from darkness for the prisoners, to proclaim the year of the LORD's favor and the day of vengeance of our God, to comfort all who mourn, and provide for those who grieve in Zion— to bestow on them a crown of beauty instead of ashes, the oil of gladness instead of mourning, and a garment of praise instead of a spirit of despair."

Scripture says this about Jesus: "But he was pierced for our transgressions, he was crushed for our iniquities; the punishment that brought us peace was upon him, and by his wounds we are healed" (Isaiah 53:5). Receive His forgiveness for yourself but also release that person who has offended you.

Jesus offers a crown of beauty instead of ashes, the oil of gladness instead of mourning, a garment of praise instead of a spirit of heaviness. You might be feeling the burden of bitterness right now, but you don't have to. Jesus wants to lift that burden from you.

Memorize IT!
Matthew 6:14: Jesus said, "For if you forgive men when they sin against you, your heavenly Father will also forgive you."

53

Ask forgiveness of others

The third principle is to quickly ask forgiveness of others. Proverbs 6:2–5 says, "If you have been trapped by what you said, ensnared by the words of your mouth, then do this, my son, to free yourself, since you have fallen into your neighbor's hands: Go and humble yourself; press your plea with your neighbor! Allow no sleep to your eyes, no slumber to your eyelids. Free yourself, like a gazelle from the hand of the hunter, like a bird from the snare of the fowler."

If you've blown it and you know it, don't allow your pride to tell you it doesn't matter. No. Rather go to the person who you've offended and ask for forgiveness. Jesus said, "But I tell you that anyone who is angry with his brother will be subject to judgment. …. Therefore, if you are offering your gift at the altar and there remember that your brother has something against you, leave your gift there in front of the altar. First go and be reconciled to your brother, then come and offer your gift" (Matthew 5:22–24). Even if your brother doesn't choose to forgive you, you can rest in the confidence that you're forgiven by God and you've done what God has asked you to do (read 1 John 1: 9).

Remember, God wants to bless you through this process. He wants to free you from the hurt and bitterness that come with unforgiveness. So forgiveness is a source of blessing not only for the other person but also for you!

Remember IT!

Write out a prayer asking God to help you understand and apply one thing from this lesson:

_____

_____

_____

_____

_____

_____

_____

Main points:
1. We must release or forgive others for the offenses and sins they've committed against us.
2. When we have offended others, we need to quickly go to them and ask for forgiveness. .

Apply IT!

1. Allow the Spirit of God to remind you of persons who you need to forgive (e.g., father, spouse, friend).
2. Through prayer and God's power, release and liberate the person who has offended you.
3. If you need to pray a similar prayer that you prayed in the last lesson, do so now. "Heavenly Father, I choose to forgive _____ [name of person] for _____[name of offense]."
4. Allow the Spirit of God to remind you of persons who you have offended (e.g., family members, friends or brothers).
5. Write those names that God reveals. Pray about the action that you need to take (e.g., when and how you're going to approach them, etc.

The Power of the Cross Over Sin and Satan

I n C.S Lewis' *Chronicles of Narnia*, the white witch of Narnia and her odd assortment of animal subjects relished their brutal murder of Aslan, the great lion. Edmund had unwittingly sold himself as a slave to the white witch with no way to escape his fate. Aslan offered himself in exchanged for Edmund and the white witch accepted. The white witch and her subjects rejoiced while killing Aslan thinking they had won the war. But in reality they only won a battle. Aslan died, but he came back to life to win the war.

At the cross, Jesus triumphed over sin and Satan. Satan seemed to defeat Him while He hung on the cross, but Jesus triumphed over the cross and rose again. And He's coming back again to fully finish the work He started.

The cross highlights God's power and triumph over the enemy. Through the cross God displayed His power in weakness. Paul said, "For the message of the cross is foolishness to those who are perishing, but to us who are being saved it is the power of God" (1 Corinthians 1:18).

Jesus carried our sins on the cross

On the cross Jesus took our place and paid the required price for sin. Scripture says, "But he was pierced for our transgressions, he was crushed for our iniquities; the punishment that brought us peace was upon him, and by his wounds we are healed. We all, like sheep, have gone astray, each of us has turned to his own way; and the LORD has laid on him the iniquity of us all" (Isaiah 53: 5, 6b). The good news is that the price has already been paid. We can't add to what has already been accomplished.

Scripture declares "God made him who had no sin to be sin for us, so that in him we might become the righteousness of God" (2 Corinthians 5:21). The Bible is full of good news because of the cross.

Try IT!

Read the following Scriptures and write out the benefits of Christ's death on the cross for us:

Romans 5:1

_____

_____

2 Corinthians 5:19

_____

_____

John 3:18

_____

_____

1 Corinthians 1:30

_____

_____

Hebrews 2:14–15

_____

_____

A dead person ceases all activity. The Greenville County, South Carolina, Department of Social Services once mistakenly sent a letter to a dead person. It said: "To whom it may concern: Your food stamps will be stopped effective immediately, because we have received notice that you passed away. You may reapply if there is a change in your circumstances." But the fact is that Death is irreversible.

Because of what Jesus did on the cross, we need to see ourselves as dead to sin and now committed to live for Jesus. Paul said, "I have been crucified with Christ and I no longer live, but Christ lives in me. The life I live in the body, I live by faith in the Son of God, who loved me and gave himself for me" (Galatians 2:20). Scripture says that we also have become dead to sin and this world through our identity with Christ. We no longer desire the things the world declares significant.

Try IT!

Read Romans 6:11–14.
What is Paul saying about our relationship to sin?

_____

_____

_____

How can you apply this in your own life?

_____

_____

_____

_____

_____

The cross and resurrection gives us power over Satan and his demons

Some people believe that Satan and his demons are imaginary figures, invented by creative minds. But Jesus acknowledged Satan's power. Jesus waged war against the devil while on earth. John calls the devil the god of this world (1 John 5:19). He's the one who deceives the inhabitants of this world. He blinds the minds of those who don't believe (2 Corinthians 4:4).

Try IT!

True or false:
☐ We should be worried about Satan and his power.
☐ We have overcome Satan and his demons through the blood of Jesus.
☐ Satan is called the god of this world.

Satan and his demons are just as real today as they were back then. One of Satan's key tactics, in fact, is to deceive people into thinking he's only a cartoon character with red horns and a pitchfork. One internet blogger wrote, "Is Satan really as bad as they say he is? I mean he's been played by so many well known actors (such as Rodney Dangerfield, Harvey Keitel, and Al Pacino) in such lovable roles." This blogger was simply reflecting the wide spread perception—encourage by Satan himself—that Satan and demons are imaginary characters like Santa Claus and the Easter Bunny.

Do IT!

Claim Christ's power through His death on the cross to overcome any area in your life in which Satan and his demons might be influencing you. Ask Jesus to take control and drive out any demonic influences over your life.

The craftiness of the enemy

Satan and his demons are masters of deception. They control the glitter of this world and all of its deception. And they are constantly deceiving people. Paul said, "In order that Satan might not outwit us. For we are not unaware of his schemes" (2 Corinthians 2:11). God wants us to be aware of Satan's schemes, so that we don't fall into his traps. The very first sin, in fact, took place when Satan tempted Adam and Eve to eat of the forbidden fruit when God strictly told them not to do so (Genesis 3:1–5).

Try IT!

Read Matthew 4:3,7.
How did Satan tempt Jesus in the wilderness?

_____

_____

_____

_____

_____

What are some of the ways Satan tempts you?

_____

_____

_____

_____

_____

_____

_____

_____

Memorize IT!
1 John 4:4: "Because the one [God] who is in you is greater than the one [Satan] who is in the world."

The Bible says that we need to be alert to Satan's schemes. 1 Peter 5:8 says, "Be self-controlled and alert. Your enemy the devil prowls around like a roaring lion looking for someone to devour." John the apostle said, "But woe to the earth and the sea, because the devil has gone down to you! He is filled with fury, because he knows that his time is short" (Revelation 12:12b).

Try IT!

Read Colossians 2:13–15.
What did God do for us because we've believed in Jesus?

_____

_____

_____

How can you apply these verses to overcome the devil?

_____

_____

_____

_____

_____

_____

Christ's triumph over demonic powers

Yet, the good news is that Jesus triumphed over Satan and his demons on the cross. I'm sure Satan and his demons were gloating and reveling in their victory. "We have him where we want him," they must have thought when Jesus hung on the cross. But God in His eternal wisdom was doing something far greater. Christ's death on the cross and His resurrection signaled Satan's eternal defeat.

Jesus disarmed Satan and his demons by dying on the cross. You are now free. Satan no longer has power over you. You can walk in victory because of what Jesus has done on the cross for you.

Try IT!

Read Revelation 12:7–9.
What is Satan doing now, according to these verses?

_____

_____

_____

How have Satan and his demons been attacking you? How can you fight back?

_____

_____

_____

_____

_____

_____

_____

And greater is the Jesus who is in you than Satan. John says, "because the one [God] who is in you is greater than the one [Satan] who is in the world" (1 John 4:4). The blood of Jesus on the cross gives protection and power (Revelation 12:11).

Remember IT!

What had the most impact for you in this lesson?_____

_____

_____

_____

_____

_____

Main points:
1. Christ on the cross conquered sin and Satan.
2. Christ took our sins on the cross and now freely offers forgiveness.

Apply IT!

1. Reflect on what Jesus has done on the cross for you.
2. Confess any area not under control of Christ. Receive Christ's forgiveness.
3. Rebuke Satan's claim to every area of your life saying, "Satan in the name of Jesus, I command you to leave _____ [name the area of your life]."

The Power of the Cross to Heal Emotional Wounds

During the first part of the 20th century, J. C. Penney presided over an empire of over 1,700 stores. At the time he owned the country's largest chain of department stores, but all that changed in 1929 when the Great Depression struck the country. Penney had overextended himself and had borrowed heavily to finance many of his ventures. Banks requested his loans sooner than anticipated and Penney couldn't make the payment schedules. Constant and unrelenting worry began to take a toll. "I was so harassed with worries that I couldn't sleep, and developed an extremely painful ailment," he said.

Penney checked himself into the Kellogg sanitarium at Battle Creek, Michigan. He was constantly tormented by periods of hopelessness and despair. His very will to live was rapidly eroding. "I got weaker day by day. I was filled with despair, unable to see even a ray of hope. I felt that I hadn't a friend left in the world, that even my family had turned against me."

When Penney felt that this night would be his last, he wrote farewell letters to his wife and son. Yet, Penney awakened the next morning, surprised to be alive. Making his way down the hallway of the hospital, he could hear singing coming from the little chapel where a devotional service was held each morning. Going into the chapel, he listened to the singing, the reading of Scripture, and the prayer. The particular hymn was

Be not dismayed whate'er betide, God will take care of you;
Beneath His wings of love abide, God will take care of you.
God will take care of you, through every day, o'er all the way;
He will take care of you, God will take care of you.

"Suddenly something happened," he said. "I can't explain it. I can only call it a miracle. I felt as if I had been instantly lifted out of the darkness of a dungeon into a warm, brilliant sunlight. I felt as if I had been transported from hell to Paradise. I felt the power of God as I had never felt it before."

In a life-transforming instant Penney knew that God loved him and was there to help. "From that day to this, my life has been free from worry," he declared. "The most dramatic and glorious twenty minutes of my life were those I spent in that chapel that morning."

Try IT!

Read Romans 8:31–39.
What is the main theme of these verses?

_____

_____

_____

Why is knowing that God loves us so critical in healing emotional wounds?

_____

_____

_____

_____

_____

_____

God wants to heal you mentally, emotionally and spiritually

God wants to heal past emotional struggles. He wants to work in us and renew us. God's will is for our inner self to be renewed by His Spirit. Scripture talks about being controlled by the the "new self." This new way of life brings peace and liberty. Some think that living for God will hinder their own personal freedom. The truth is that giving your life to Jesus and living for Him will make you whole. God will heal emotions, memories, and failed dreams.

Try IT!

Read Colossians 3:9–10.
How is the new self different from the old self, according to these verses?

_____

_____

_____

What are the changes you've seen in your own life since becoming a Christian?

_____

_____

_____

_____

_____

_____

_____

Christ's death on the cross not only forgives sin but also offers the healing of emotions and pain (Luke 19:10). Referring to Jesus, Scripture says, "Surely he took up our infirmities and carried our sorrows, yet we considered him stricken by God, smitten by him, and afflicted. But he was pierced for our transgressions, he was crushed for our iniquities; the punishment that brought us peace was upon him, and by his wounds we are healed" (Isaiah 53:4–5).

Much of our hurt affects our inner person, causing painful emotions, bad attitudes, fears and physical illness. God wants to liberate us from resentments, rejection, depression, guilt, fear, and condemnation.

Do IT!

Ask the Holy Spirit to reveal areas in which you've felt rejection. Then pray to Jesus Christ to heal you of fears and memories. Christ's death on the cross provides the healing you need for all emotional hurt you have experienced.

Dealing with rejection

Racism is an example of extreme rejection. White slave owners rejected any claim that blacks were human beings. Even today, certain groups reject all historical evidence of the Holocaust, where Nazi Germany attempted to exterminate out the Jewish race.

Most people have not experienced such extreme rejection, but all of us have felt some form of rejection. Some people bounce back from rejection and live as if nothing even happened. Then there are some who have experienced a deeply emotional, damaging, and life altering experience. Because they have psychologically internalized the experience, they have become emotionally wounded and feel devastatingly degraded.

Try IT!

Read Ezekiel 16:4, 6.
Even though Ezekiel is talking about God's work in the nation Israel, how can you apply these verses to God's work in your own life?

_____

_____

_____

_____

_____

_____

_____

_____

_____

People often build walls, trying to protect themselves from the painful feeling of rejection. These walls, however, often serve as a reminder of rejection. Many people try to cope with rejection silently. They shuffle through life like a zombie, struggling to avoid further pain. God wants to be their refuge and strength, a safe place to experience His love and acceptance—something we all need.

Rejection, in fact, is one of life's most painful emotions. Deep rejection might be caused by abandonment or lack of love from parents. Perhaps it came about through the divorce of parents, a parent's death, parent's suicide, or parent's destructive habits (abuse, adultery, or violence). Many couples had such high hopes for their marriage only to find themselves mirred in an ugly divorce. Rejection in marriage discolors every aspect of our lives and causes both spouses to feel condemned, rejected, and depressed. Some people suffer from ethnic rejection. Their lives are gravely affected by the bias of others.

Without God's healing power, many live with paralyzing fear, compulsive spending, paranoia, paralyzing shyness, obesity, distrust, confusion, inability to admit errors, laziness, or depression.

Try IT!

Reflect on areas where you've felt rejected in your life. How did you deal with it?

_____

_____

_____

_____

_____

_____

_____

Give those feelings of rejection to God, allowing Him to fill you with His love.

God's great love and healing power

Because of God's great love and kindness, He seeks to heal you and make you whole. That is good news! Scripture says, "In all their distress he too was distressed, and the angel of his presence saved them. In his love and mercy he redeemed them; he lifted them up and carried them all the days of old" (Isaiah 63:9). God and God alone can heal and set you free. He's able to heal the emotionally wounded and make whole everyone who needs His help.

Try IT!

Read Psalm 139:15–16.
How long has God known us intimately?

_____

_____

How does God's intimate knowledge of you encourage you? Discourage you?

_____

_____

_____

_____

_____

_____

_____

_____

_____

God knows us and loves us. Scripture says, "For he chose us in him before the creation of the world to be holy and blameless in his sight" (Ephesians 1:4). God knew your plight before you were even born. He loves you and cares for you. You're very special to Him, so you can go to Him with all your needs and wants. He loves you and has a perfect plan for you. Christ is our healer. He himself "was despised and rejected by men, a man of sorrows, and familiar with suffering. Like one from whom men hide their faces he was despised, and we esteemed him not" (Isaiah 53:3). He is the only one who truly understands us and is able to deal with the difficulties that we face. He loves you and cares for you. You are so special to Him, and He wants to make your life so special.

Memorize IT!

Isaiah 53:5: "But he was pierced for our transgressions, he was crushed for our iniquities; the punishment that brought us peace was upon him, and by his wounds we are healed."

How to receive God's healing

How do you receive God's healing? First, place your faith in Jesus to heal you. Receive His love and forgiveness in your life. You can't really care for others as Jesus wants unless Jesus has first reached into your own life.

Now go back to those past, painful rejections and allow God to work in you. Think of those people and situations that have hurt you and caused you grief. Believe that God calls you to forgive them. God will work through you and He'll work in you.

Think of those moments in your life where you felt pain, rejection, humiliation, and embarrassment. Ask the Spirit of God to show you areas of your life that need healing. If possible, write them down.

G. Campbell Morgan was a famous preacher of the nineteenth century. In 1888, he was one out of 150 people seeking ordination in the Methodist Church. He passed the doctrinal examinations. But then he faced the trial sermon. In a cavernous auditorium that could seat more than 1,000 sat three ministers and 75 others who came to listen.

When Morgan stepped into the pulpit, he did his best. But two weeks later Morgan's name appeared among the 105 REJECTED for the ministry that year.

Morgan was very discouraged. He wrote in his diary, "Everything seems very dark." Then he wired a one-word letter to his father: "Rejected."

But the very next day, his father wrote him back. And he said, "Rejected on earth. Accepted in heaven. Dad."

Later on, Morgan said that it was his dad's letter that helped him make it through this difficult time in his life. Morgan bounced back from this and he was ordained in the Congregational Church. He went on to become one of the greatest preachers of that century.

You are accepted by heaven. You may have felt rejected by people, but know that God accepts you and loves you. You will never be rejected by God. He'll always love you.

Remember IT!

What had the most impact for you in this lesson?_____

_____

_____

_____

_____

_____

_____

_____

_____

_____

Main points:

1. God knows all about every rejection you've experienced.
2. Jesus is able to heal every emotional wound and turmoil.

Apply IT!

1. Name those area of rejection or pain in your life (ask the Holy Spirit to reveal those areas).
2. Allow God's grace and love to touch those difficult areas in your life. Allow him to heal you. Receive His fullness.

The Power of the Cross Over Strongholds

Randy, an elementary school principal, was a great encouragement to me. As a leader in his church, he encouraged new ideas and believed the best about people. I talked with Randy at a church evangelism outreach on Halloween night. Randy was in charge of one of the booths and like always, he was smiling and reaching out. That night I talked with Randy for the last time. Just a few weeks later, he dropped dead of a massive heart attack.

Clogged arteries—whether through heredity or poor eating habits—is one of the major reasons for sudden heart attacks like the one Randy experienced. Sometimes when the normal flow of blood stops, the heart ceases to function.

Many believers in Christ appear happy and even attend church meetings regularly. Yet, underneath the outward signs of success and joy are spiritual blockages, very much like clogged arteries. We call these blockages strongholds.

What is a stronghold?

The simple definition of a stronghold is a heavily fortified place. The word is used both positively and negatively in Scripture. Positively, Scripture says "The LORD is a refuge for the oppressed, a stronghold in times of trouble" (Psalms 9:9). Negatively, Scripture says, "For though we live in the world, we do not wage war as the world does. The weapons we fight with are not the weapons of the world. On the contrary, they have divine power to demolish strongholds" (2 Corinthians 10:3–4).

The word picture in 2 Corinthians 10:3–4 seems to refer to the conquest of Canaan. The Israelites took the Land but not ALL of it was under their control. Certain strongholds were under control of the pagan nations and remained holdouts for many years, even centuries. God told them that unless they dealt with those enemy strongholds, they would be taken captive by them. Even today if we don't demolish strongholds such as pornography, anger, bitterness, etc., those areas will begin to control us. Even though we've given our life to Christ, some areas may be "out of control." Satan then takes ground in those areas that are not under Christ's control.

For example, Satan begins to build astrongholds in our lives in those areas that we haven't submitted to Jesus. Satan uses these ungodly strongholds to take more and more control of our lives.

Try IT!

Identify any areas of your life that are out of control.

_____

_____

_____

_____

_____

_____

_____

_____

Present those areas to God, asking Him to heal you and guide you.

Satan and his demons look for entry points

What kind of stronghold are we referring to? The Bible gives us several examples. Scripture says, "'In your anger do not sin': Do not let the sun go down while you are still angry, and do not give the devil a foothold" (Ephesians 4:26). Anger then would be an example of a stronghold.

Then there's the stronghold of bitterness. Scripture says, "See to it that no one misses the grace of God and that no bitter root grows up to cause trouble and defile many" (Hebrews 12:15). These are examples of slavery that bind people and make them the slaves of sin.

Christ wants to give us abundant life but Satan wants to destroy. Satan tries to take away in order to destroy. He tries to divide and conquer.

Renounce the stronghold of deception

Satan is the master deceiver. He knows how to deceive people. He's raised up false cults and religious counterfeits to trap people. Paul said, "But I am afraid that just as Eve was deceived by the serpent's cunning, your minds may somehow be led astray from your sincere and pure devotion to Christ. For if someone comes to you and preaches a Jesus other than the Jesus we preached, or if you receive a different spirit from the one you received, or a different gospel from the one you accepted, you put up with it easily enough" (2 Corinthians 11:3–4). Like counterfeit money, false cults and religious systems often have many similar elements of the real thing. The difference is that Satan hooks people into false systems that snares them and holds them in bondage.

Deuteronomy 18:10–11 says, "Let no one be found among you who … practices divination or sorcery, interprets omens, engages in witchcraft, or casts spells, or who is a medium or spiritist or who consults the dead." According to these verses in Deuteronomy, what is God's attitude toward these practices?

In the New Testament, Paul teaches that witchcraft is a work of the flesh (Galatians 5:20) and those who practice it will not inherit the kingdom of God (Galatians 5:21). "Anyone who does these things is detestable to the LORD" (Deuteronomy 18:12a). No Christian should participate in a false cult or practice teaching that is contrary to God's Word.

God is a holy God. He requires that we only serve him. After this lesson, you'll have the opportunity to fill out the spiritual inventory and have the opportunity to renounce past or present involvement in false cults or other demonic practices.

God wants to deliver us from deception. He wants us to free our spiritual lives to walk in liberty. To do this, we must renounce participation in false cults. Remember that Jesus already died to free us from all bondage. No further price must be paid! We must claim Christ's rightful Lordship over each rebellious idea.

Try IT!

Confess any area of your life where sin continues to reign:

_____

_____

Whom do you need to forgive?

_____

_____

Experience freedom from the stronghold of addictive habits

Addictions are commonplace in our society. So many people have fallen prey to the bondages of addiction. Because of our sinful nature, we sometimes fall into temptation that causes us to sin, and this sin becomes a foothold for the devil to control our lives. Often addictions are interrelated. That is, one sin attracts the other sin (e.g., alcoholism might find common ground with pornography).

Paul said, "Therefore do not let sin reign in your mortal body so that you obey its evil desires" (Romans 6:12). He also says to the Galatian church, "You, my brothers, were called to be free. But do not use your freedom to indulge the sinful nature; rather, serve one another in love" (Galatians 5:13).

Do IT!
*Name a particularly addictive sin. Give it to Jesus
and know that He bore that sinful area on His cross.
Ask the Spirit of God to free you from it.*

Choose humility to conquer the stronghold of pride

Ronald Reagan recalled an occasion when he was Governor of California and made a speech in Mexico City: "After I had finished speaking, I sat down to rather unenthusiastic applause, and I was a little embarrassed. The speaker who followed me spoke in Spanish—which I didn't understand—and he was being applauded almost every paragraph. To hide my embarrassment, I started clapping before everyone else and longer than anyone else until our ambassador leaned over and said, 'I wouldn't do that if I were you, he's interpreting your speech.'"

Although this was quite an innocent mistake, pride is one of the deadliest and oldest sins. Pride led Satan, once a beautiful angel, to fall from his heavenly dwelling.

Pride is one of those sins that God hates; Proverbs 16:18 says, "Pride goes before destruction, a haughty spirit before a fall." A proud person says, "I can do it by myself. I don't need help from anyone—not even God." The opposite of pride is humility. God is attracted to those who walk in humility.

Memorize IT!
James 4:10: "Humble yourselves before the Lord, and he will lift you up."

Renounce the stronghold of curses; bless others

A curse is a pattern of evil and disobedience that is passed down through family habits, customs, and cultures. Satan and his demons use habits and patterns of sin to enslave the next generation.

Jeff Tunnell lives in Big Bear City, CA. He was born and raised in Springfield, IL His dad was an alcoholic who, in his drunken state, would physically abuse Jeff's mother and oldest brother. This brother, Clifford Joe (bearing his father's name) swore he'd never become like his dad. However, in the year the dad died of alcoholism, CJ became an alcoholic. This fostered the continuance of the curse and CJ has been divorced three times. His eldest son recently died in a Navy pilot training accident, but because of CJ's angry, alcoholic lifestyle, he missed the funeral. Jeff, on the other hand, received Christ as a teenager, became a strong follower of Jesus, and eventually became a pastor. God helped Jeff to break the sinful patterns (curses) that followed his brothers. All of Jeff's children are following Jesus. The pattern of evil has been broken in Jeff's family but continues in CJ's life and lineage.

Sinful generational patterns are often passed on to future generations. I'm referring to lifestyle patterns that often continue as the norm in each generation—adultery, unfaithfulness, abuse, abandonment, divorce, hate, vices, misery, and violence. God said to His people as they lived among idol worshiping nations, "You shall not bow down to them or worship them; for I, the LORD your God, am a jealous God, punishing the children for the sin of the fathers to the third and fourth generation of those who hate me" (Exodus 20:5b). Those who refuse God's ways end up following the world's patterns.

Evil patterns might start small and grow larger over time. Some parents, for example, place a "curse" on their children by labeling them with phrases such as, "you're just a loser," "you're an alcoholic, just like you're father," "you're ugly," etc. These labels become so ingrained in succeeding generations that apart from God's intervention, they become the norm. If these patterns have been a part of your background, or are currently present, Jesus wants to free you and turn your life around.

The good news is that God wants you to reverse this trend. The Bible teaches us that there is a heritage of blessing that goes beyond genetics and has to do with the decisions and the spiritual direction that each family chooses. By repentance and commitment to Christ, we can choose a new lifestyle that will bless future generations (2 Corinthians 5:17).

We need to read the rest of Exodus 20:6: "… but showing love to a thousand generations of those who love me and keep my commandments."

Christ's overcoming power

On the cross Jesus took upon Himself every curse that we or others have brought on us. He became a curse for us. Galatians 3:13–14 says: "Christ redeemed us from the curse of the law by becoming a curse for us, for it is written: "Cursed is everyone who is hung on a tree."

Jesus set us free from the curse pronounced by the Law. Those who persist living under the Law (trying to be perfect through good works) after what Christ has done are reverting to life under a curse

Try IT!

Read 2 Corinthians 5:21.
What did Jesus become for us?

_____

_____

_____

_____

_____

How can you apply this truth right now?

_____

_____

_____

_____

_____

_____

_____

_____

_____

_____

_____

_____

Breaking curses

To overcome the pattern of curses and disobedience you should:

1. Identify recurring patterns of sin and disobedience in your family.
2. Pray for your family and friends. People in Scripture often confessed the sins of their ancestors.
3. Confess any sin or ungodly vows (promises) you have made to follow sinful patterns or satanic practices.
4. Renounce the authority of a particular sin over your life and the life of your family.
5. Forgive people who hurt you, cursed you or disappoint you.
6. Make a commitment to bless others rather than curse them.

You might want to pray a prayer like this: *"Heavenly Father, I believe that on the cross Jesus took every curse that could ever be spoken or brought against me and my family. So I ask you now to release me from every curse over my life. I also claim total release of my family from all of these curses. In the name of Jesus I specifically break the curses of _____. By faith I receive total release and I thank you for it."*

Try IT!

Read Jeremiah 14:20.
Notice that Jeremiah acknowledges that his ancestors had sinned.
How can you apply this to your situation?

_____

_____

_____

_____

_____

The Bible calls us to reverse the flow of curses by blessing those who curse us. 1 Peter 3:9 says, "Do not repay evil with evil or insult with insult, but with blessing, because to this you were called so that you may inherit a blessing."

Try IT!

Read Romans 12:14, 21.
What is Paul's point in these verses?

_____

_____

How can you apply these principles in your own life?

_____

_____

_____

_____

_____

_____

_____

_____

_____

_____

_____

Remember IT!

What is one thing from this lesson you want to share with someone close to you?

_____

_____

_____

_____

_____

_____

_____

Main points:
1. Jesus died and rose again to release us from sin.
2. Christians can fall prey to sin's strongholds, allowing Satan to hold areas in their lives.

Apply IT!

1. Take time to mark the spiritual freedom inventory included in Appendix 3 of this book. Please check any areas that you have experienced in the past or are dealing with in the present If your family has experienced or is experiencing any of these areas, please circle the appropriate box.

2. No one else needs to read this questionnaire. What you write is between you and the Lord. Be completely honest, allowing the Holy Spirit to bring to your mind every areas where He wants to bring healing.

The Power of the Cross Over Sickness and Death

A long-standing church member met with the pastor to plan for her funeral—whenever that might take place. She wanted to make sure her favorite hymns were sung, that she was buried by her husband and that she wouldn't burden her kids with paying for her coffin. When it seemed that they had covered everything, she paused, looked up at pastor with a twinkle in her eye, and said, "One more thing, pastor, when they bury me, I want my old Bible in one hand and a fork in the other." "A fork?" the pastor was sure he had not heard right. "Why do you want to be buried with a fork?" She replied, "I have been thinking about all the great dinners I have been to down through the years, and one thing sticks in my mind. At those really nice get-togethers, when the meal was almost finished, the hostess would come by and take the plate and whisper, 'You can keep your fork.' And do you know what that meant? Dessert was coming!"

"That's exactly what I want people to talk about at my funeral. When they walk by my casket and see the fork, I want them to turn to one another and say, 'Why the fork'? That's when I want you to say, 'the fork represents that the best is yet to come!'"

Philippians 3:20–21 says, "But our citizenship is in heaven. And we eagerly await a Savior from there, the Lord Jesus Christ, who, by the power that enables him to bring everything under his control, will transform our lowly bodies so that they will be like his glorious body." The best is yet to come when we find ourselves in heaven with a new body in the presence of Jesus Christ.

The cross helps overcome disease and sickness

Our healing of sin took place on the cross, but there's provision for physical healing through the wounds of Jesus Christ as well. This doesn't mean that Christ's death automatically will provide healing as some groups allege. God is sovereign and heals those He chooses.

Try IT!

Read 3 John 2.
What is John praying for?

_____

_____

How can you apply this prayer to your own life?

_____

_____

_____

_____

_____

_____

_____

_____

Sickness, in general, is the consequence of the presence of evil in the world and at times God intervenes in the form of miraculous physical healing. Scripture says, "Surely he took up our infirmities and carried our sorrows, ... and the LORD has laid on him the iniquity of us all" (Isaiah 53:4a, 6b). Verse five of that same passage says, "But he was pierced for our transgressions, he was crushed for our iniquities; the punishment that brought us peace was upon him, and by his wounds we are healed" (Isaiah 53:5).

Do IT!

Pray for someone who needs healing right now. If you personally have physical ailments, ask your pastor or coach to pray for you.

People today are in dire of need for healing of high blood pressure, mental problems, cancer, heart problems, alcoholism, or generational sickness on either side of the family. You can pray and believe God for His healing touch. He's able and willing to heal.

Try IT!

True or false:
- ☐ God will heal all people who pray hard enough.
- ☐ We can't force God to heal people because He's sovereign.
- ☐ The root of sickness is sin and the presence of evil in the world.

The cross and the resurrection gives us victory over death

Soon after the discovery of the New World, Europeans began making the long journey across the ocean in hopes of finding a new life. Some wanted adventure. Some wanted religious freedom. Others came in search of gold. A Spanish conquistador by the name of Ponce de Leon and his men were the first Europeans to explore Puerto Rico, parts of Mexico, and Florida. In his quest to find gold, he met many native peoples who told him of a spring that bubbled up out of the ground. It was said that this spring had magical powers. Anyone who drank the water would be healed of any disease and would never die. Their bodies would once again be youthful. It was appropriately called the "Fountain of Youth." De Leon searched all his life for this fountain; but, in 1521 a poisoned arrow ended his quest.

Memorize IT!

Hebrews 2:14,15: "Since the children have flesh and blood, he too shared in their humanity so that by his death he might destroy him who holds the power of death—that is, the devil— and free those who all their lives were held in slavery by their fear of death."

God does heal today, but the ultimate healing only comes through death. Paul says in 1 Corinthians 15:50–54, " I declare to you, brothers, that flesh and blood cannot inherit the kingdom of God, nor does the perishable inherit the imperishable. Listen, I tell you a mystery: We will not all sleep, but we will all be changed— in a flash, in the twinkling of an eye, at the last trumpet. For the trumpet will sound, the dead will be raised imperishable, and we will be changed. For the perishable must clothe itself with the imperishable, and the mortal with immortality. When the perishable has been clothed with the imperishable, and the mortal with immortality, then the saying that is written will come true: 'Death has been swallowed up in victory.'"

On the cross, Jesus conquered death. He took away the devil's power over death. No longer will we die eternally because we have the guarantee of the resurrection. Scripture says, "Since the children have flesh and blood, he too shared in their humanity so that by his death he might destroy him who holds the power of death—that is, the devil—and free those who all their lives were held in slavery by their fear of death" (Hebrews 2:14, 15).

Satan came to kill and destroy. He introduced sin into the world and death through sin, but Jesus came to give us abundant and eternal life (John 10.10b). Yet, look what Paul says about death. "The last enemy to be destroyed is death" (1 Corinthians 15:26). And Scripture says, "Then death and Hades were thrown into the lake of fire. The lake of fire is the second death" (Revelation 20:14).

Try IT!

Read 2 Corinthians 5:6–8.
What was Paul's preference?

_____

_____

_____

What kind of feelings do you have when you think about death?

_____

_____

_____

_____

_____

_____

_____

_____

_____

_____

_____

_____

Remember IT!

What truth from this lesson impacted you the most?

_____

_____

_____

_____

_____

_____

_____

Main points:

1. Sickness and death are part of the human experience. On the cross Jesus died not only for our sin, but also to make provision for our physical healing.

2. God wants us to pray boldly for physical healing, but He is sovereign and chooses to heal some and not others.

3. Ultimately, the greatest healing will take place in heaven when God gives us a new body.

Apply IT!

1. If you are sick or bound by the fear of death, pray that God heals you and releases you from all fear (if possible, ask someone to pray for you).

2. Has God ever healed you of a sickness? Meditate on the fact that you can freely go to Him for all problems and difficulties.

Living in Victory

For two years I lived in Pasadena, California, the home of the famous New Year's Day Rose Parade. One year during the parade, a beautiful float suddenly sputtered and coasted to a halt. It was out of gas. The whole parade was held up until someone could get a can of gas over to the float and get it moving again. The amusing thing was that this float represented the Standard Oil Company! Even with its vast oil resources, the company's float had run out of gas. In much the same way, Christians often neglect their spiritual maintenance, and although they have been filled with the Holy Spirit, they need to be refilled.

The filling of the Spirit

In Ephesians 5:18, Paul wrote: "Do not get drunk on wine, which leads to debauchery. Instead, be filled with the Spirit." In the original Greek, the phrase "be filled" is a present-tense verb to denote that the filling of the Holy Spirit is not a one-time event but a continual experience. Scripture says that we must be continually filled with the Spirit.

The word filling seems awkward when referring to the Holy Spirit's work in our lives. The Spirit of God is not a liquid, like water. He does not fill a person the way cold milk fills a cup. The Holy Spirit is God—He is one in essence with the Father and the Son—but He is also a distinct person and has all the attributes of a person. That is why we refer to the Holy Spirit as the third person of the Trinity.

Because the Holy Spirit is a person, it makes more sense to talk about the Holy Spirit's control or guidance in our lives, rather than His filling of our lives. Holy Spirit-led is a good way to look at our response to His control. A person who is filled with the Spirit is led by the Spirit—led in a gentle, loving way. A Spirit-led person allows the Holy Spirit to direct and guide every decision, plan and activity. Because the world, the flesh and the devil oppose the Spirit-controlled lifestyle, we need to be filled and renewed continually.

Try IT!

Read Ephesians 4:30.
What does this verse say about the personality of the Holy Spirit?

_____

_____

In what areas do you sometimes grieve the Spirit of God and what can you do to change this?

_____

_____

_____

_____

_____

_____

_____

_____

Who should receive the promise of the Spirit?

The Bible says that the promise of God's Spirit is for everyone (Acts 2:39). No one can become a Christian, in fact, without receiving the Holy Spirit (John 3:3). Yet, not everyone is filled with the Spirit. The filling of the Spirit is something we have to ask for (Ephesians 5:18).

Some have used the analogy of the pilot light on the stove. It's always on, but if you really want it to cook, you have to turn it up. The Holy Spirit is in every believer but we have to ask Him to control our lives.

Try IT!

True or false:

☐ All believers have the Spirit within them at new birth.

☐ God promises to fill with the Spirit all those who ask.

☐ All believers will automatically be filled with the Spirit.

The Spirit empowers us to serve

I was first filled with the Holy Spirit in early 1974. In September 1973, approximately four months earlier, I had received Jesus by praying the prayer of salvation in my bedroom. At that moment in September 1973, I became a Christian, but I lacked power.

During those initial months as a Christian, I was afraid to proclaim to others my newfound faith in Christ. I was in my last year of high school and desperate to become bold about sharing my faith. My lack of spiritual power led me to attend a miracle service of Shekinah Fellowship that gathered in a Foursquare church in downtown Long Beach, California.

Although I responded to the general altar call after the service, I knew exactly what I needed. I longed for power and boldness so that I would not be ashamed of my Christian faith. The elders at Shekinah prayed for me to receive the fullness of the Holy Spirit. Change was evident the very next day. My life was totally transformed from that night onward. I began to carry my Bible with me everywhere, setting it down on the right corner of each classroom desk at Millikan High

School. I wanted people to know that I was a believer—and I had the confidence to prove it. The Shekinah Fellowship experience, however, was not enough. I needed repeated fillings of the Spirit's grace and power.

Try IT!

Not everyone responds the same way to God's filling. Here are a few responses:

- An overwhelming sense of God's love (Romans 5:5; Eph. 3:14–20).
- Empowerment to serve (Acts 6:3–5,10).
- Performing signs and wonders (Acts 2:4–11, 31; 5:12–16).
- Some people (not all) will speak in tongues (Acts 8:16–18; 10:46).

What is one of the ways that you respond when the Spirit ministers to you?

_____

_____

_____

_____

_____

_____

_____

No need to doubt God's promise

I heard about a particular church whose electric organ stopped halfway through the hymn singing during Sunday-morning worship. The organist was not quite sure what to do. Fortunately, the pastor was in control of the situation, and he asked the congregation to follow the Scripture reading, intending to lead them in prayer, as well.

As he read the Scripture portion, an usher quietly approached the organist and handed her a note that read, The power will be on after the prayer.

The power comes on after prayer! The Scripture makes it crystal clear that God is exceedingly willing to fill us with His Holy Spirit. All we need to do is pray. Jesus taught His disciples that the heavenly Father would freely give the Holy Spirit to anyone who would simply ask (Luke 11:13). But Jesus wasn't content to talk about the Holy Spirit on just one occasion. Throughout the gospels, Jesus heightened expectations among His disciples about the promised Holy Spirit.

Try IT!

Read John 14: 15–17.
What does Jesus call the Holy Spirit?

_____

_____

How does the Holy Spirit counsel you?

_____

_____

_____

_____

_____

_____

_____

_____

The Holy Spirit is eager, willing and excited to work in us and flow through us. Ask and you will receive! Simply ask for the Holy Spirit's fullness. The power comes on after prayer.

How do we receive the Holy Spirit?

Once we realize how much the Holy Spirit wants to bless and fill us, we need to spend time in His presence and then ask Him to fill us again and again. Jesus tells us in John 7:37 to thirst for the Spirit. And even if you don't have that thirst right now, you can ask God to create a thirst in you (Rev. 22:17). Jesus also invites us to come to Him to receive the Spirit.

Try IT!

Read John 7:37–39.
What does Jesus ask us to do?

_____

_____

How can you apply this to your life this week?

_____

_____

_____

_____

_____

_____

_____

The last thing is to ask. Jesus said, "So I say to you: Ask and it will be given to you. … Which of you fathers, if your son asks for a fish, will give him a snake instead? Or if he asks for an egg, will give him a scorpion? If you then, though you are evil, know how to give good gifts to your children, how much more will your Father in heaven give the Holy Spirit to those who ask him!" (Luke 11:11–13). God wants us to ask and He will fill us.

> **Memorize IT!**
> **Ephesians 5:18: "Do not get drunk on wine, which leads to debauchery. Instead, be filled with the Spirit."**

Living in the Spirit

We've talked about being filled with the Holy Spirit, but just as important is living in the Spirit on a daily basis.

Hopefully, you've been set free as you've gone through this guide. In one sense, being set free is easy, staying set free is harder! To a healed paralytic, Jesus said, "See, you are well again. Stop sinning or something worse may happen to you" (John 5:14). To the woman caught in adultery, he said, "Then neither do I condemn you. Go now and leave your life of sin" (John 8:11).

By now, you have probably recognized that Jesus has been at work in your life. Now it's important to walk daily with Him. Please continue studying and growing. Paul said, "Since we live by the Spirit, let us keep in step with the Spirit" (Galatians 5:25). Allow me to suggest several ways to "keep in step with the Spirit."

First, you need to master the discipline of spending daily quiet time with Jesus Christ. The next book in this series is called *Grow! Deepen Your Relationship with Christ*. Even if your church is using a different training book, please read my book, *An Appointment with the King* (1-888-344-CELL). I believe it's the most important book I've written because it highlights how to spend daily, quality time with Jesus Christ.

To keep in step with the Spirit, make sure you actively participate in a cell group and the worship celebration service. Hebrews 10:25 says, "Let us not give up meeting together, as some are in the habit of doing, but let us encourage one another—and all the more as you see the Day approaching."

If you are following all five books of this equipping track, please notice that each book has a corresponding action step.

First step: *Live! Experience Christ's Life*

Action step: be baptized

Second step: *Encounter! Receive Christ's Freedom*

Action step: break from sinful habits

Third step: *Grow! Deepen your Relationship with Christ*

Action step: have a daily quiet time with Jesus

Fourth step: *Share! Make Christ Real to Others*

Action step: befriend non-Christians and share the gospel message

Fifth step: *Lead! Guide a Small Group to Experience Christ*

Action step: facilitate a cell group or be part of a multiplication team

The above are helpful in moving you forward as you grow in Christ. Even if you are using different material, the most important thing is to keep in step with the Spirit and continue progressing in the Christian life.

Do IT!

1. Read Romans chapter 8 and apply what Paul says about living in the Spirit.
2. Determine to take the next step listed above (step 3) in Christian growth.

Above all, seek to live a Christ-honoring life. He's coming soon and what a joy it will be to hear him say, "Well done, good and faithful servant" (Matthew 25:23).

Remember IT!

What stood out to you in this lesson?

_____

_____

_____

_____

_____

_____

_____

Main points:

1. The Holy Spirit is a person and wants to control us. The filling of the Spirit is a continual experience of allowing the Holy Spirit to control us.

2. If a person desires the Spirit's fullness, comes to God, and asks Him for the Holy Spirit, the Holy Spirit will fill that person.

3. The daily walk in the Spirit is just as important as the filling of the Spirit.

4. Keep moving forward in the Christian life. Take the next step in following Him.

Apply IT!

1. When you're alone, ask the Holy Spirit to fill you.

2. Pinpoint the area(s) where you are most easily tempted or sidetracked. Think about what you need to do to avoid the trap of these temptations. Then pray like this, "Lord, I choose obedience to You in every area and every decision in my life."

How to Coach Someone Else Using this Material

Many churches will teach this material in a group setting. This is the normal way to use the material, but it's not the only way. If you choose to teach a group of people, outlines and PowerPoints are provided for all five equipping books on a CD. Purchase this CD at www.cellchurchsolutions.com or by calling 1-888-344-CELL.

Another way to train someone is to allow the person to complete each lesson individually and then ask someone of the same gender to coach him or her. The coach would hold the "trainee" responsible to complete the lesson and share what he or she is learning.

I believe in multiple methods for teaching material. The fact is that not everyone can attend group-training meetings. But the person still needs training. Coaching is a great option.

Coaching the trainee through the material

Ideally, the coach will meet with the trainee after each lesson. At times, however, the trainee will complete more than one lesson and the coach will combine those lessons when they meet together.

The coach is a person who has already gone through the material and is now helping someone else in the training process. Additionally a coach must have:

- a close walk with Jesus.
- a willing, helpful spirit. The coach doesn't need to be a "teacher." The book itself is the teacher—the coach simply holds the trainee accountable with asking questions and prayerful encouragement.

I recommend my book, How to be a Great Cell Group Coach, for additional understanding of the coaching process (this book can also be purchased on the CCS web site or by calling 1-888-344 CELL). The principles in How to be a Great Cell Group Coach apply not only to coaching cell leaders but also to coaching a trainee. I recommend the following principles:

- Receive from God. The coach must receive illumination from Jesus through prayer so he has something of value to give to the trainee.

- Listen to the person. The coach's job is to listen to the trainee's answers. The coach should also listen to the trainee's joys, struggles, and prayer concerns.

- Encourage the trainee. Often the best thing the coach can do is point out areas of strength. I tell coaches to be a fanatic for encouragement. We all know our failures and have far too much condemnation hanging over us. Encouragement will help the trainee press on and look forward to each lesson. Try to start each lesson by pointing out something positive about the person or about what he or she is doing.

- Care for the person. The person might be struggling with something above and beyond the lesson. The material might bring out that specific problematic area. The best coaches are willing to touch those areas of deep need through prayer and counsel. And it's one hundred percent acceptable for the coach to simply say, "I don't have an answer for your dilemma right now, but I know someone who does." The coach can then go to his or her own coach to find the answer and bring it back the next week.

- Develop/train the person. Hopefully the person has already read the lesson. The goal of the coach is to facilitate the learning process by asking specific questions about the lesson.

- Strategize with the trainee. The coach's job is to hold the trainee accountable to complete the next lesson and/or finish the current one. The coach's main role is to help the trainee sustain the pace and get the most out of the material.

- Challenge the person. Some think that caring is good but confronting is wrong. The word care-fronting combines the two and is what the Bible promotes. If we truly care, we'll confront. The Spirit might show you areas in the trainee's life that need to come under the Lordship of Christ. The best approach is to ask for permission. You might say, "Tom, may I have permission to speak to you about something I'm noticing?" After the person gives you permission, you can then tell him what the Lord is laying on your heart.

First session

When the coach meets with the trainee, the Holy Spirit will guide the session. Creativity and flexibility should reign. I do recommend, however, the following principles:

- Get to know the person. A great way to start is to use the Quaker questions. This will help you to warm up to each other. After the first week, the coach can open in prayer and simply ask about the trainee's life (e.g., family, work, studies, spiritual growth, etc.)

Quaker questions
1. Where did you live between the ages of 7–12?
2. How many brothers and sisters did you have?
3. What form of transportation did your family use?
4. Whom did you feel closest to during those years?

- Be transparent. Since you've already completed this training material, share your experiences with the trainee. Transparency goes a long way. Great coaches share both victories and struggles.

"Coaching questions" to use each week

A great coach asks lots of questions and listens intently. The goal is to draw the answers from the trainee so that he or she applies the material to daily living. Key questions to ask each time are:
1. What did you like best about the lesson(s)?
2. What did you like least about the lesson(s)?
3. What did you not understand?

4. What did you learn about God that you didn't know previously?
5. What do you personally need to do about it?

The coach doesn't have to ask each of the above questions, but it is good to get into a pattern, so the trainee knows what to expect each week.

Pattern to follow each week
1. Prepare yourself spiritually before the session begins.
2. Read the lesson in advance, remembering the thoughts and questions you had when you went through the material.
3. Start the session in prayer.
4. Ask the coaching questions.
5. Trust the Holy Spirit to mold and shape the trainee.
6. Close in prayer.

Instructions for Leading an Encounter Retreat

Two essential items stand out in preparation for an Encounter Retreat: prepared worship and diligent schedule planning.

Worship and Prayer

It's essential to have prepared worship. It's ideal to have a worship leader. But if not, worship songs and prayer spots must be interwoven into the entire Encounter Retreat.

The worship leader should also be prepared to play worship songs when called upon, play music in the background, and especially to prepare about seven sets of worship (about three worship songs per set) to play at times throughout the Encounter. I normally ask the worship leader to play a worship set before I present each of the lessons. I sometimes ask the worship leader to play a set in the middle of a longer session.

Remember that prayer and worship are the environment that make Encounter retreats effective.

Both you and the prayer team should remember to pray before the Encounter begins.

Using this book

Each member should have a copy of this book to follow along during the teaching time. The "teaching material" that I offer on CD will closely follow this book and will compliment it.

This book offers more personal illustrations and exercises while the teaching material on the CD will be in an outline format.

Various Schedules

If you're using the group retreat format for the Encounters, I've noted at least three options. If you have more time and want to linger in God's presence, go for the three-day schedule (Friday night to Sunday afternoon). The extended two-day schedule starts on Friday night and ends on Saturday night. The shortened two-day schedule starts on Friday night and ends at 5 p.m. on Saturday.

Three-day schedule: This schedule begins in the evening on Friday (say, 7:30 p.m.) and ends Sunday afternoon (or perhaps returns on Sunday morning in time to go to a later church service). If you do the three-day schedule, spread the lessons out, allowing much more time for application at the end of each lesson. Give the people a two to five hour afternoon break-time on Saturday (depending on how much was covered on Friday and Saturday morning).

Extended two-day schedule: This schedule also begins in the evening on Friday and ends Saturday night after the last session (perhaps finishing at 9 p.m.). This schedule also allows for more application time and an afternoon break of 1-2 hours. This is also a preferred schedule.

Shortened two-day schedule: Many churches in western countries do the shortened two-day schedule because of time constraints. I've held and directed various encounters using the shortened two-day schedule and they've worked very well. Yet, I've also learned that I have to manage the flow of the lessons. Thus, if you decide to use this schedule, I strongly recommend diligent planning and sticking to the schedule. Here's my recommendation:

- Friday from 7 p.m. to 9:30 p.m. (complete lessons 1-3)
- Saturday from 9 a.m. to 5 p.m.
    - -9 a.m. to 12 p.m. Complete lessons 4, 5 and part of 6 (up to the spiritual inventory part)
    - -12 p.m.: lunch
    - -1 p.m.: Start with the spiritual inventory application exercise of Lesson 6 (filling out spiritual inventory and meeting with accountability partner) and then complete lesson 7-8
    - -5 p.m.: Dismiss in prayer

Spiritual Inventory

Please check any areas that you have experienced in the past or are dealing with in the present. If your family has experienced or is experiencing any of these areas of struggle or sin, please circle the appropriate box. No one else needs to read this questionnaire. What you write is between you and the Lord. Be completely honest, allowing the Holy Spirit to bring to your mind every areas where He wants to bring healing.

1. What kinds of sins or situations have been recurring in your family (parents, grandparents, etc).
   - ☐ Adultery
   - ☐ Fornication
   - ☐ Rape
   - ☐ Suicides
   - ☐ Physical infirmities. Write what kinds _____
   - ☐ Cheating, stealing
   - ☐ Poverty
   - ☐ Divorce
   - ☐ Mental sickness
   - ☐ Other _____

2. Which of the following have been present in your life?
   - ☐ I have been cursed by members of my family
   - ☐ I was born in fornication and adultery
   - ☐ I wasn't wanted from the moment of conception and during the pregnancy
   - ☐ My father or mother died during the first years of my life

☐ I was an orphan, or my parents abandoned me
☐ My parents divorced or separated before I became an adult
☐ I was treated cruelly during my childhood
☐ I was abused sexually as a child
☐ I have very painful memories that are reoccurring
☐ I wished that I had never been born or was not alive today
☐ I have uncontrollable habits, such as: _____

3. Emotional problems that I can't control:
   ☐ Anger
   ☐ Worry
   ☐ Fear
   ☐ Excessive depression
   ☐ Negativity
   ☐ Fear of death
   ☐ Fear of failure
   ☐ Fear of the future
   ☐ Rejection
   ☐ Fear of loneliness
   ☐ Suicidal thoughts
   ☐ Bitterness
   ☐ Lack of forgiveness
   ☐ Other _____

4. I have anger problems with those of the opposite sex (or perhaps of the same sex)

5. I'm tempted or have inclinations toward:
   ☐ Homosexuality
   ☐ Lesbianism
   ☐ Pornography
   ☐ Other _____

6. The following thoughts continually torment me:
   ☐ Guilt, condemnation (even after having confessed my sins to God)
   ☐ I find it very difficult to forgive people—even myself

- ☐ I have resentment against God
- ☐ I carry deep resentments and/or prejudice toward certain people or groups of peoples for no apparent reason (e.g., church, Jews, blacks, indigenous people, etc.)
- ☐ I desire to curse God and do things like destroy Bibles

7. Mark down whether you have participated or have had contact with:
   - ☐ At some time participated in false religious cults such as; Jehovah's Witnesses, Mormons, Hare Krishna, etc.
   - ☐ Witchcraft
   - ☐ Spiritual games (Ouija, etc.)
   - ☐ Spiritists
   - ☐ Astrology
   - ☐ Hypnosis
   - ☐ Black or white magic
   - ☐ Extraterrestrial trips
   - ☐ Sexual spirits
   - ☐ Palm readers
   - ☐ Contact with "beings of light"
   - ☐ Spiritual guides
   - ☐ Aliens
   - ☐ New age
   - ☐ I have felt the presence of evil around me
   - ☐ Other _____

8. Other
   - ☐ At some time, I have had an abortion or participated in one
   - ☐ I was consecrated to a Saint, a virgin, or a dead family member
   - ☐ I've received images of good luck in my business, home, family, etc.
   - ☐ I've participated in oriental religious activity
   - ☐ I have made blood pacts with someone or a group of person

Index

A

Abraham,10, 11, 12, 14
Acts, 14
Adam,37
addictions,5, 14, 54
alcoholism,54, 56, 65
altar,12, 14, 31, 71
ancestors,59

Appointment with the King,75

B

Baptism,3
Bible,2, 81
bitterness, 25, 27, 29, 30, 31, 52, 53
bondage,5, 18, 19, 23, 29, 53, 54

C

Canaan,51
Christ, 1, 81
Chronicles of Narnia,33
Coaching,79, 81
curse,10, 55, 56, 58, 59, 60, 87

D

David,13, 14, 18
deception,36, 53, 54
dryness,28

E

emotions,29, 43, 44, 45
encouragement, 80
enemy, 33, 36, 38, 52, 66
Eve,37, 53
expectations,8, 9, 73

F

foothold,53, 54
forgetting,29
forgiveness,14, 17, 19, 20, 21, 23, 23,
    26, 30, 31, 32, 40, 48, 86

G

G. Campbell Morgan,48
generation,55, 56
generational sickness,65
grieve,30, 70

H

heal,8, 9, 14, 17, 43, 44, 46, 48, 50,
        52, 65, 66, 68
Holy Spirit, 81, 82

I

iniquities,18, 30, 33, 44, 48, 65

J

Jacob,12, 14
Jesus, 3, 14, 80, 79

L

love,5, 19, 2
1, 26, 27, 41, 45, 46, 48, 49, 50, 54,
        57, 21, 46, 72

M

Matthew,18, 19
memories,29, 43, 44, 86
Moses,9, 8, 9, 14

P

pattern,19, 59, 82, 55, 56
Penney,41, 42
physical healing,64, 65, 68
pornography,52, 54
prayer,32
Pride,55
principle,8, 9, 31
promise,10, 11, 22, 71, 72

Q

Quaker, 81

R

Randy,51
rejection,27, 44, 45, 46, 48, 50
relationship,14
repentance,17, 18, 56
Ronald Reagan,55

S

Samaria,13
Sickness,63, 65, 68
Sovereign LORD,30
spiritual, 82
stronghold,51, 53, 54, 55
suffering, 27, 47

T

transformation,14, 19
trust,22, 28, 29
Tunnell,56

U

unforgiveness,14, 25, 26, 28, 31

V

victory,3